The Disrupter's Handbook: How to Create Change Through Protest

Table of Contents

Introduction

Protests have been a powerful force for social and political change throughout history. From the Civil Rights Movement in the United States to the Arab Spring in the Middle East, protests have been used to challenge unjust systems, demand equal rights and opportunities, and bring attention to issues that are often ignored by those in power. While the tactics and strategies of protest have evolved over time, the underlying goals and motivations remain the same: to effect change and create a more just and equitable world.

Protests come in many forms, from peaceful demonstrations and marches to more confrontational actions such as sit-ins and strikes. They can be organized by individuals, grassroots groups, or established organizations, and they can target a wide range of issues, from economic inequality and political corruption to climate change and police brutality.

One of the most powerful aspects of protests is their ability to bring attention to issues that might otherwise be overlooked or ignored. By gathering in public spaces and drawing media attention, protests can raise awareness about issues that might not be covered by mainstream media or discussed in political circles. This can be especially important for marginalized communities, who often face systemic discrimination and lack access to political power.

Protests can also be a way for individuals to come together and build solidarity around a shared cause. By connecting with others who share their values and beliefs, protesters can build networks of support and create a sense of community that can be empowering and transformative.

However, protests can also be met with resistance and violence, both from the police and from counter-protesters. This can be especially true in authoritarian regimes, where dissent is often met with brutal repression. As such, it is important for protesters to be mindful of their safety and to take steps to protect themselves and others during demonstrations.

Despite the risks, protests continue to be a powerful force for social and political change. They provide a way for individuals and communities to speak truth to power, to challenge the status quo, and to demand a more just and equitable world. As such, protests remain an important tool for activists and organizers around the world, and they will likely continue to be a key part of social and political movements for years to come.

Why protests are important

Protests have long been a tool for individuals and groups to demand change and challenge the status quo. From the civil rights movement to the fight for women's suffrage, protests have been instrumental in shaping the course of history.

Protests are important for several reasons. First and foremost, they give a voice to marginalized groups who may otherwise be ignored or silenced by those in power. Protests serve as a way for people to collectively express their dissent and demand change, whether it be in response to social, economic, or political issues.

In addition, protests can help to raise awareness about an issue and build public support for a cause. By bringing attention to an issue through media coverage and public demonstrations, protests can help to change public opinion and increase pressure on decision-makers to take action.

Protests also provide an opportunity for people to come together and build a sense of community around a shared cause. This can be especially important for marginalized groups who may otherwise feel isolated or powerless. By organizing and participating in protests, people can connect with others who share their values and work together towards a common goal.

Furthermore, protests can be a powerful way to challenge unjust laws and policies. When individuals and groups take to the streets to demand change, they can pressure those in power to reevaluate their decisions and take action to address injustices.

Moreover, protests can serve as a catalyst for political and social change. History has shown us that protests have been instrumental in achieving major social and political reforms, such as the end of apartheid in South Africa, the legalization of same-sex marriage in the United States, and the overthrow of authoritarian regimes around the world.

Finally, protests can serve as a way to hold those in power accountable for their actions. When decision-makers fail to address the concerns of their constituents, protests can send a powerful message that their actions will not be tolerated. This can lead to increased transparency and accountability in government, as well as greater responsiveness to the needs of the people.

Protests are important because they give a voice to marginalized groups, raise awareness about important issues, build community, challenge unjust laws and policies, catalyze social and political change, and hold those in power accountable. As such, protests are a vital tool for those seeking to create a more just and equitable society.

The power of collective action

The power of collective action is a fundamental principle behind the success of protests. Protests are often organized and carried out by groups of individuals who share a common cause or goal. By working together towards a shared objective, individuals can amplify their voices and create a greater impact than they would be able to alone.

One of the key benefits of collective action is the ability to mobilize large numbers of people. When individuals come together to protest, they send a powerful message to those in power that their concerns are widely shared and cannot be ignored. This can be especially effective in creating pressure on decision-makers to take action.

In addition, collective action can help to build momentum and sustain a movement over time. By creating a sense of community around a shared cause, individuals can provide each other with support and encouragement to continue working towards their goals. This can help to overcome obstacles and setbacks, and ensure that the movement remains strong and effective.

Moreover, collective action can be a powerful tool for promoting social change. By bringing attention to an issue and mobilizing large numbers of people, protests can help to shift public opinion and build support for a cause. This can be especially important in situations where decision-makers are resistant to change, as protests can create pressure to reconsider their positions.

Furthermore, collective action can help to create a sense of empowerment and agency among individuals. When people come together to protest, they are able to assert their rights and demand change in a way that may not be possible as individuals. This can help to build confidence and self-esteem, and create a sense of ownership and responsibility for creating positive change.

Finally, collective action can help to create a legacy of activism and social change. When individuals come together to protest and achieve their goals, they can inspire others to do the same. This can help to create a culture of activism and social responsibility that can have lasting effects on society.

In conclusion, the power of collective action is a key factor in the success of protests. By mobilizing large numbers of people, building momentum and sustaining a movement over time, promoting social change, creating a sense of empowerment and agency, and inspiring a legacy of activism, collective action can be a powerful tool for creating positive change in society.

Defining Your Cause

Identifying the issue you want to address

Identifying the issue you want to address is a crucial step in planning and carrying out a successful protest. In order to effectively communicate your message and generate public support, it is important to clearly define the issue you want to address and articulate why it is important.

One of the first steps in identifying an issue is to conduct research and gather information about the problem you want to address. This may involve reviewing news articles, academic studies, or other relevant sources of information. It is also important to consider the perspectives and experiences of those who are most directly impacted by the issue, such as members of marginalized communities or those who have been personally affected by the issue.

Once you have a clear understanding of the issue, it is important to define your goals and objectives for the protest. This may involve identifying specific policy changes you would like to see, or broader social or cultural changes you hope to inspire. It is important to set realistic goals and objectives that are achievable and meaningful.

Another important aspect of identifying the issue is to consider the broader social and political context in which it exists. This may involve considering the historical roots of the issue, or examining the ways in which it intersects with other forms of oppression or inequality. Understanding the broader context can help to identify potential allies and partners in the struggle, as well as potential barriers or obstacles to success.

In addition to identifying the issue itself, it is also important to consider the potential consequences of taking action. This may involve assessing the risks and benefits of different tactics or strategies, and considering the potential impact on different stakeholders, including those who may be opposed to your cause.

Finally, it is important to develop a clear and compelling message that effectively communicates the issue and your goals to a wider audience. This may involve developing a slogan or tagline, creating visual materials such as posters or flyers, or using social media to spread your message. It is important to ensure that your message is accessible and inclusive, and that it speaks to a broad range of people who may be impacted by the issue.

Identifying the issue you want to address is a critical step in planning and carrying out a successful protest. By conducting research, setting clear goals and objectives, considering the broader social and political context, assessing potential risks and consequences, and developing a clear and compelling message, you can effectively communicate your message and generate public support for your cause.

Narrow issue or broad

Whether it is better to have a narrowly defined issue or a broadly defined problem depends on the specific goals and objectives of the protest, as well as the broader social and political context in which it exists.

Narrowly defined issues can be effective in focusing attention on a specific policy or practice that is causing harm. By identifying a specific issue and articulating why it is important to address, protestors can create a sense of urgency and demand immediate action. This can be especially effective in situations where there is a clear solution to the problem, or where there is already broad public support for addressing the issue.

On the other hand, broadly defined problems can be effective in highlighting the systemic or structural nature of a social or political issue. By articulating the ways in which different forms of oppression and inequality intersect and reinforce one another, protestors can build a broader movement for social change. This can be especially effective in situations where there is no easy or immediate solution to the problem, or where there is resistance to change among decision-makers.

Another consideration is the potential impact on different stakeholders. Narrowly defined issues may be more likely to generate immediate support from those who are directly impacted by the issue, as well as from allies who share similar goals. However, they may be less effective in mobilizing support from those who are not directly impacted, or who may be less familiar with the issue. Broadly defined problems may be more likely to generate interest and support from a wider range of stakeholders, as they speak to broader social and political issues that impact many different groups.

In addition, the broader social and political context should also be considered. For example, in situations where there is a broader movement for social change that is focused on a specific issue, it may be more effective to align with that movement and work towards a narrowly defined goal. On the other hand, in situations where there is resistance to change or where there is a need to build broader public support, a broadly defined problem may be more effective in generating momentum and sustaining a movement over time.

In conclusion, whether it is better to have a narrowly defined issue or a broadly defined problem depends on a variety of factors, including the specific goals and objectives of the protest, the potential impact on different stakeholders, and the broader social and political context in which it exists. Ultimately, the most effective approach will depend on the specific situation and the strategic decisions made by organizers and protestors.

Articulating your goals and demands

Articulating your goals and demands is a critical step in planning and carrying out a successful protest. It is important to clearly communicate your message and objectives in order to mobilize support, generate media attention, and put pressure on decision-makers to take action.

One of the first steps in articulating your goals and demands is to identify the specific policy or practice that you want to change. This may involve conducting research, consulting with experts or community members, or gathering information through direct action or protest. It is important to clearly define the problem and articulate why it is important to address.

Once you have identified the problem, it is important to set clear and achievable goals for the protest. This may involve identifying specific policy changes that you would like to see, or broader social or cultural changes that you hope to inspire. It is important to set realistic goals that are achievable and meaningful, and that are grounded in the experiences and perspectives of those who are most directly impacted by the issue.

In addition to setting goals, it is important to articulate specific demands that you are making of decision-makers or other stakeholders. This may involve developing a list of concrete actions that you would like to see taken, such as changes to laws or policies, increased funding for specific programs, or other forms of tangible support. It is important to ensure that your demands are clear, specific, and actionable, and that they are grounded in the experiences and perspectives of those who are most directly impacted by the issue.

Another important aspect of articulating your goals and demands is to develop a clear and compelling message that effectively communicates your message and objectives to a wider audience. This may involve developing a slogan or tagline, creating visual materials such as posters or flyers, or using social media to spread your message. It is important to ensure that your message is accessible and inclusive, and that it speaks to a broad range of people who may be impacted by the issue.

Finally, it is important to consider the broader social and political context in which your protest is taking place. This may involve considering the perspectives and interests of different stakeholders, as well as the potential consequences of taking action. It is important to develop a strategy that takes into account the risks and benefits of different tactics and approaches, and that is designed to maximize the impact of your protest.

Articulating your goals and demands is a critical step in planning and carrying out a successful protest. By identifying the specific policy or practice that you want to change, setting clear and achievable goals, articulating specific demands, developing a clear and compelling message, and considering the broader social and political context, you can effectively communicate your message and generate public support for your cause.

Understanding your audience

Understanding your audience is a crucial step in planning and executing a successful protest. Whether you are trying to raise awareness about an issue, mobilize public support, or put pressure on decision-makers to take action, it is important to understand who your audience is and how to effectively communicate your message to them.

Your audience may include a wide range of people, including supporters of your cause, neutral observers, and even those who are opposed to your message. It is important to consider the perspectives and experiences of these different groups, and to develop a strategy that speaks to their concerns and interests.

One important aspect of understanding your audience is to consider their level of knowledge and awareness about the issue you are protesting. For example, if you are protesting against a specific policy or practice, it is important to consider whether your audience understands the impact of that policy or practice on the community. You may need to provide additional information or context to help them understand why the issue is important and why action is needed.

Another important aspect of understanding your audience is to consider their values and beliefs. Different groups may have different priorities, concerns, and interests, and may respond differently to different types of messaging or tactics. For example, if you are protesting an environmental issue, you may need to tailor your messaging to different audiences, such as emphasizing the impact on public health for some groups and the impact on local ecosystems for others.

It is also important to consider the communication channels and platforms that are most effective in reaching your audience. For example, social media may be an effective way to reach younger audiences, while traditional media may be more effective in reaching older audiences. You may also need to consider language barriers or other factors that could impact your ability to effectively communicate with certain groups.

Finally, it is important to consider the potential consequences of your protest on your audience. For example, if you are engaging in civil disobedience or other forms of direct action, you may risk alienating some members of your audience or losing public support. It is important to weigh the potential risks and benefits of different tactics and approaches, and to develop a strategy that is designed to effectively communicate your message while minimizing negative impacts on your audience.

In conclusion, understanding your audience is a critical step in planning and executing a successful protest. By considering the perspectives and experiences of different groups, tailoring your messaging and tactics to their concerns and interests, and considering the potential consequences of your actions, you can effectively communicate your message and mobilize public support for your cause.

Building a Strong Foundation

Building a team

Building a team is essential to the success of any protest. A well-organized and motivated team can help you plan and execute your protest, and can provide the support and resources you need to achieve your goals.

The first step in building a team is to identify individuals who are passionate about your cause and are committed to making a difference. This may include friends, family members, colleagues, or members of your community who share your values and beliefs. You can also reach out to existing organizations or activist groups that are working on similar issues and see if they would be interested in partnering with you.

Once you have identified potential team members, it is important to establish clear roles and responsibilities for each person. This may include tasks such as organizing logistics, fundraising, outreach and communication, media relations, and legal support. Each member of your team should have a clearly defined role and understand what is expected of them.

Communication is key to building a strong and effective team. Regular meetings, email updates, and online collaboration tools can help ensure that everyone is on the same page and that progress is being made towards your goals. It is also important to establish clear lines of communication and decision-making processes, so that everyone understands how decisions are being made and can provide input when needed.

In addition to building a core team, it is important to reach out to supporters and volunteers who can help amplify your message and increase your impact. This may include individuals who are not able to commit to a long-term role, but who are willing to help with specific tasks, such as spreading the word on social media, attending rallies, or providing financial support.

Finally, it is important to create a positive and inclusive team culture that celebrates diversity and encourages open communication and collaboration. Building a team that is reflective of the communities you are fighting for can help ensure that your message resonates with a wide range of people, and can help build long-term support for your cause.

Building a strong and effective team is essential to the success of any protest. By identifying passionate and committed individuals, establishing clear roles and responsibilities, communicating effectively, reaching out to supporters and volunteers, and creating an inclusive team culture, you can effectively plan and execute your protest and achieve your goals.

Establishing roles and responsibilities

Establishing clear roles and responsibilities is an important aspect of organizing a successful protest. Every member of your team should have a specific role to play in order to ensure that the protest is well-planned, well-executed, and achieves its goals.

One of the first steps in establishing roles and responsibilities is to identify the different areas of work that need to be done. This may include logistics, outreach and communication, fundraising, media relations, legal support, and more. Once you have identified the different areas of work, you can start to assign specific roles to individual team members based on their strengths, skills, and interests.

It is important to clearly define the responsibilities of each team member and to ensure that everyone understands what is expected of them. This may involve creating job descriptions or task lists for each role, outlining specific deadlines and goals, and establishing clear lines of communication and decision-making.

Regular communication and collaboration are essential to ensuring that everyone is on the same page and that progress is being made towards your goals. This may involve regular meetings or check-ins, as well as the use of online collaboration tools such as shared documents, calendars, and project management software.

In addition to establishing roles and responsibilities for your core team members, it is important to involve volunteers and supporters in your protest planning process. This may involve creating opportunities for volunteers to take on specific tasks, such as distributing flyers or organizing transportation, and ensuring that they have the resources and support they need to be effective.

In conclusion, establishing clear roles and responsibilities is essential to the success of any protest. By identifying the different areas of work that need to be done, assigning specific roles to individual team members, and ensuring that everyone understands what is expected of them, you can effectively plan and execute your protest and achieve your goals.

Securing resources and funding

Securing resources and funding is a crucial step in organizing a successful protest. Without adequate resources, it can be difficult to plan and execute your protest effectively, and your message may not reach as many people as you would like.

One of the first steps in securing resources and funding is to create a budget for your protest. This may involve identifying the different expenses associated with your protest, such as permits, equipment, transportation, food and water, and any necessary legal fees. Once you have a clear understanding of your budget, you can start to explore different funding sources to help cover your expenses.

One potential source of funding is crowdfunding. There are a variety of online crowdfunding platforms that can help you raise money for your protest, such as Kickstarter, GoFundMe, or Crowdfunder. When setting up your crowdfunding campaign, be sure to clearly communicate your goals and objectives, and explain how the funds will be used to support your cause.

Another option is to reach out to local organizations or businesses that may be interested in supporting your cause. This may involve creating a sponsorship package that outlines the benefits of supporting your protest, such as increased exposure and positive brand association. You may also consider partnering with other activist groups or community organizations to pool resources and increase your impact.

In addition to securing funding, it is also important to secure resources such as equipment, transportation, and other supplies. This may involve reaching out to local businesses or organizations to request donations of these items, or considering renting or purchasing them yourself.

Finally, it is important to ensure that your use of resources and funding is transparent and accountable. This may involve keeping detailed records of your expenses, providing regular updates to your supporters and donors, and being prepared to answer any questions or concerns that may arise.

Securing resources and funding is a critical step in organizing a successful protest. By creating a budget, exploring different funding sources, reaching out to local organizations and businesses, and being transparent and accountable in your use of resources, you can effectively plan and execute your protest and achieve your goals.

Organizing and Planning Your Protest

Choosing a date and location

Choosing the right date and location for your protest is an important aspect of organizing a successful and impactful event. The location and date can greatly impact the turnout, visibility, and media coverage of your protest.

When choosing a location, consider the accessibility and visibility of the area. It is important to choose a location that is easily accessible for participants, and that is highly visible to the public and media. Public parks, city halls, and busy intersections are popular locations for protests, as they are often highly visible and accessible.

In addition to accessibility and visibility, consider the symbolic significance of the location. Choosing a location that is directly related to the issue you are protesting can add a powerful and meaningful element to your protest. For example, if you are protesting police brutality, you may choose to protest outside a police station or courthouse.

When choosing a date, consider factors such as the weather, other events happening in the area, and holidays. It is also important to consider the availability of participants, as well as any important dates related to your cause. For example, if you are protesting climate change, you may choose to hold your protest on Earth Day.

It is also important to obtain any necessary permits or permissions for your chosen location and date. Contact local authorities to find out what permits or permissions may be required for your protest, and be sure to obtain them well in advance of the event.

Finally, be prepared to have contingency plans in case of unexpected circumstances, such as inclement weather or unexpected counter-protests. Have a backup location and date in mind, and be prepared to communicate any changes to participants and the media.

In conclusion, choosing the right date and location is a crucial aspect of organizing a successful protest. By considering factors such as accessibility, visibility, symbolism, and permissions, you can choose a date and location that maximizes turnout and impact, and effectively communicates your message to the public and media.

Creating a timeline and schedule

Creating a detailed timeline and schedule is essential for ensuring that your protest runs smoothly and achieves its goals. A well-organized timeline and schedule can help you keep track of key deadlines and tasks, allocate resources effectively, and ensure that all participants are aware of their roles and responsibilities.

The first step in creating a timeline and schedule is to identify the key milestones and deadlines associated with your protest. This may include tasks such as securing permits, booking equipment and transportation, and promoting your event through social media and other channels.

Once you have identified these key tasks, create a timeline that outlines the specific dates by which each task should be completed. Be sure to build in enough time to account for unexpected delays or issues that may arise.

Next, create a detailed schedule for the day of the protest. This may include tasks such as setting up equipment, coordinating transportation for participants, and assigning roles and responsibilities to volunteers and organizers. Be sure to include breaks and rest periods in your schedule to help ensure that participants remain energized and engaged throughout the event.

When creating your timeline and schedule, it is important to communicate these details clearly and consistently to all participants. Make sure that everyone involved in the protest is aware of the key deadlines and tasks, and understands their role in the event. This may involve holding regular meetings or conference calls with participants, or using social media and other channels to communicate updates and reminders.

Finally, be prepared to adjust your timeline and schedule as needed. Unexpected issues or delays may arise, and it is important to be flexible and responsive in order to ensure that your protest runs smoothly and achieves its goals.

In conclusion, creating a detailed timeline and schedule is a critical aspect of organizing a successful protest. By identifying key milestones and deadlines, creating a detailed schedule for the day of the event, communicating these details clearly to participants, and being prepared to adjust your plans as needed, you can effectively plan and execute your protest, and achieve your goals.

Developing a messaging and communication strategy

Developing a messaging and communication strategy is critical for the success of your protest. Your messaging and communication strategy will help you effectively communicate your goals, demands, and message to participants, the public, and the media.

The first step in developing your messaging and communication strategy is to clearly articulate your goals and demands. Your messaging should be focused and concise, and should clearly communicate what you hope to achieve through your protest.

Once you have defined your messaging, it is important to identify your target audience. This may include potential participants, the media, elected officials, or members of the general public. By understanding your target audience, you can tailor your messaging and communication strategy to effectively reach and engage with them.

Next, identify the key messages and talking points that you want to convey. These messages should be clear, concise, and compelling, and should effectively communicate your goals and demands.

Consider using statistics, personal stories, or other evidence to support your messaging.

It is also important to consider the channels through which you will communicate your messaging. This may include social media, traditional media outlets, email, or direct mail. Consider which channels are most effective for reaching your target audience, and develop a plan for how you will use these channels to effectively communicate your message.

Finally, be prepared to adapt your messaging and communication strategy as needed. Monitor the response to your messaging, and be prepared to adjust your strategy based on feedback or changing circumstances. By being flexible and responsive, you can ensure that your messaging and communication strategy effectively communicates your goals and demands, and helps you achieve your desired outcome.

In conclusion, developing a messaging and communication strategy is critical for the success of your protest. By clearly articulating your goals and demands, identifying your target audience, developing key messages and talking points, and using effective channels to communicate your message, you can effectively engage with participants, the public, and the media, and achieve your desired outcome.

Mobilizing Support

Building coalitions and partnerships

Building coalitions and partnerships is a key element of organizing a successful protest. By bringing together diverse groups and organizations, you can amplify your message, build support, and increase the impact of your protest.

The first step in building coalitions and partnerships is to identify organizations and groups that share your goals and values. This may include advocacy groups, community organizations, faith groups, labor unions, and others. Consider reaching out to these organizations and inviting them to join your coalition.

Once you have identified potential partners, it is important to build relationships with them. This may involve attending their events, participating in their campaigns, or simply reaching out to them to learn more about their work. By building strong relationships, you can establish trust and mutual respect, and build a foundation for effective collaboration.

When building coalitions and partnerships, it is important to establish clear goals and expectations. Be sure to communicate your goals and demands clearly, and work with your partners to identify shared objectives and strategies for achieving them.

Effective communication is also critical when building coalitions and partnerships. Be sure to establish regular communication channels with your partners, and keep them informed of key developments and decisions related to your protest. This may involve regular meetings, conference calls, or email updates.

Finally, be prepared to work through challenges and conflicts that may arise when building coalitions and partnerships. It is normal for groups with different priorities and perspectives to have disagreements or conflicts. By maintaining open lines of communication, being willing to compromise, and focusing on shared goals, you can effectively work through these challenges and build a strong and effective coalition.

In conclusion, building coalitions and partnerships is an important element of organizing a successful protest. By identifying organizations and groups that share your goals and values, building strong relationships, establishing clear goals and expectations, maintaining effective communication, and working through challenges and conflicts, you can build a strong and effective coalition that can amplify your message and help you achieve your goals.

Engaging with the media

Engaging with the media is an important part of organizing a successful protest. Effective media engagement can help you reach a wider audience, increase awareness of your cause, and build support for your goals and demands.

The first step in engaging with the media is to develop a clear message that communicates your goals and demands. This message should be tailored to your target audience and should be concise, compelling, and easy to understand. Consider using statistics, personal stories, or other evidence to support your message.

Once you have developed your message, it is important to identify media outlets and journalists who may be interested in covering your protest. This may involve researching local and national media outlets, as well as journalists who cover issues related to your cause.

When reaching out to the media, it is important to be professional and respectful. Consider sending a press release or pitch letter that introduces your protest and provides key details, such as the date, time, and location of the event. Be sure to include contact information and offer to provide additional information or interviews if needed.

During the protest, designate a spokesperson or media liaison who can speak to the media on behalf of your group. This person should be well-informed about your goals and demands, and should be able to effectively communicate your message to the media. Be sure to provide the media with any materials or information they may need, such as fact sheets, press releases, or interviews with participants.

After the protest, follow up with the media and thank them for their coverage. This can help build relationships with journalists and increase the likelihood that they will cover future events related to your cause.

In conclusion, engaging with the media is an important part of organizing a successful protest. By developing a clear message, identifying media outlets and journalists, being professional and respectful, designating a spokesperson or media liaison, and following up after the protest, you can effectively engage with the media and increase awareness of your cause.

Using social media and digital tools
Using social media and digital tools can be a powerful way to mobilize support for your protest and reach a wider audience. Here are some tips for using these tools effectively:

- Choose the right platforms: There are many social media platforms available, each with its own strengths and weaknesses. Consider which platforms are most popular among your target audience, and focus your efforts on those platforms.

- Develop a strategy: Before you start posting on social media, develop a clear strategy that outlines your goals, target audience, messaging, and tactics. This will help you stay focused and ensure that your efforts are effective.

- Create compelling content: To capture people's attention on social media, you need to create compelling content that is visually appealing, informative, and easy to share. Consider using images, videos, and infographics to convey your message.

- Use hashtags: Hashtags are a powerful way to connect with people who are interested in your cause. Choose a hashtag that is memorable and easy to remember, and use it consistently across all your social media platforms.

- Engage with your audience: Social media is a two-way conversation, so it's important to engage with your audience and respond to their comments and questions. This will help you build relationships with your followers and increase engagement.

- Use digital tools: There are many digital tools available that can help you organize and promote your protest. For example, you can use event management platforms to create and promote your protest, or use digital petition platforms to gather signatures in support of your cause.

- Measure your results: To know if your social media and digital efforts are working, it's important to measure your results. Use analytics tools to track your reach, engagement, and other key metrics, and use this information to refine your strategy over time.

In conclusion, using social media and digital tools can be an effective way to mobilize support for your protest and reach a wider audience. By choosing the right platforms, developing a strategy, creating compelling content, using hashtags, engaging with your audience, using digital tools, and measuring your results, you can increase the impact of your protest and build momentum for your cause.

Preparing for the Protest

Developing a security plan

Developing a security plan is a critical step in organizing a protest, as it helps ensure the safety of participants and protects against potential risks or threats. Here are some key considerations for developing a security plan:

1. Assess potential risks: Before you can develop an effective security plan, you need to understand the potential risks and threats associated with your protest. This could include anything from counter-protesters to police violence, depending on the nature of your protest.

2. Identify security personnel: Depending on the size and nature of your protest, you may need to hire or designate security personnel to help manage and respond to potential risks. This could include private security personnel, trained volunteers, or designated marshals.

3. Develop communication protocols: It's important to establish clear communication protocols between security personnel and protest

organizers, as well as between security personnel themselves. This will help ensure that everyone is on the same page and able to respond effectively in the event of an emergency.

4. Establish physical barriers: Depending on the location of your protest, you may need to establish physical barriers to protect participants from potential threats. This could include barricades, fencing, or other types of barriers.

5. Train volunteers: If you are relying on volunteers to help with security, it's important to provide them with proper training and guidance to ensure that they are able to respond effectively in the event of an emergency.

6. Establish medical protocols: In addition to security protocols, it's important to establish medical protocols to ensure that participants receive timely and appropriate medical attention if needed. This could include designating medical personnel or setting up first aid stations.

7. Develop a contingency plan: Despite your best efforts, it's impossible to

anticipate and prepare for every potential risk or threat. Therefore, it's important to develop a contingency plan that outlines how you will respond in the event of an emergency or unexpected situation.

In conclusion, developing a security plan is a critical step in organizing a protest, as it helps ensure the safety of participants and protects against potential risks or threats. By assessing potential risks, identifying security personnel, developing communication protocols, establishing physical barriers, training volunteers, establishing medical protocols, and developing a contingency plan, you can help ensure that your protest is safe and effective.

Training marshals and volunteers

Training marshals and volunteers is a crucial component of protest organization, as it helps ensure that everyone involved is prepared to handle potential risks and respond effectively in the event of an emergency. Here are some key steps to consider when training marshals and volunteers:

1. Provide an overview of the protest: Before diving into specific training, it's important to provide marshals and volunteers with an overview of the

protest's goals, demands, and messaging. This will help them understand the context of the protest and their role in supporting it.

2. Explain the marshal role: Marshals play a critical role in managing and de-escalating potential conflicts during a protest. It's important to explain the marshal role in detail, including their responsibilities, how to communicate effectively with other marshals and organizers, and how to respond to different scenarios.

3. Review de-escalation techniques: Marshals and volunteers should be trained on effective de-escalation techniques, such as active listening, staying calm, and avoiding physical contact. They should also be prepared to intervene if necessary to prevent potential violence.

4. Discuss communication protocols: It's important to establish clear communication protocols between marshals, organizers, and other participants. This could include establishing specific radio channels, hand signals, or other forms of

communication that can be used to quickly and effectively relay information.

5. Practice scenario-based training: One of the most effective ways to prepare marshals and volunteers for potential risks is through scenario-based training. This involves simulating potential scenarios that may arise during the protest, such as counter-protesters or police confrontations, and practicing how to respond effectively.

6. Review legal considerations: Marshals and volunteers should be trained on their legal rights and responsibilities, as well as any relevant local laws or regulations related to protest activity. This will help ensure that everyone involved is able to act within the bounds of the law and avoid potential legal repercussions.

7. Provide ongoing support and resources: Finally, it's important to provide ongoing support and resources to marshals and volunteers throughout the protest. This could include access to mental health resources, debriefing sessions after the protest, or follow-up

training to help them continue building their skills.

In conclusion, training marshals and volunteers is a critical component of protest organization. By providing an overview of the protest, explaining the marshal role, reviewing de-escalation techniques, discussing communication protocols, practicing scenario-based training, reviewing legal considerations, and providing ongoing support and resources, you can help ensure that your protest is safe and effective.

Managing legal and logistical considerations

Organizing a successful protest requires careful management of legal and logistical considerations. One key step is to obtain any necessary permits or permission from local authorities, which can vary depending on the location and size of the protest. It's important to research and understand the specific requirements in your area, and to submit any necessary applications well in advance of the protest date.

Another important consideration is to plan for potential legal issues that may arise during the protest. This could include knowing your rights to free speech and assembly, understanding how to handle interactions with law enforcement, and having legal representation or support available if needed.

Logistical planning is also critical, including considerations such as transportation, parking, and restroom facilities for attendees. It's important to ensure that the protest location is accessible to attendees and that any necessary equipment, such as sound systems or signs, are readily available.

Additionally, it's important to consider any potential safety risks and plan accordingly. This could include identifying potential hazards, such as traffic or inclement weather, and developing contingency plans to address them. By carefully managing legal and logistical considerations, organizers can help ensure that their protest runs smoothly and achieves its goals.

Executing the Protest

Staging effective demonstrations

Staging effective demonstrations is essential to the success of any protest. Here are some key strategies to consider when planning a demonstration:

First, choose a location that is relevant to the issue you are protesting and that is easily accessible to your target audience. This could be a government building, a public park, or another location that is closely linked to the issue you are protesting. You should also consider the visibility of the location, as well as any potential safety concerns.

Once you have selected a location, you should focus on creating compelling visuals that will help convey your message and draw attention to your cause. This could include banners, signs, or other visual aids that clearly and concisely express your message. Be sure to choose colors and designs that are eye-catching and easy to read.

In addition to visual aids, consider using other forms of creative expression, such as music or performance art, to engage your audience and reinforce your message. This can help create a more dynamic and memorable experience for attendees.

Another important element of staging effective demonstrations is ensuring that your messaging is consistent and easy to understand. This means articulating your goals and demands clearly and concisely, and using messaging that is accessible and relatable to your target audience. Be sure to use language that is inclusive and avoids jargon or technical terms that may be confusing.

It's also important to consider logistics when staging a demonstration. This includes factors such as transportation, parking, and restroom facilities for attendees. Make sure the location is easily accessible, and that any necessary equipment, such as sound systems or podiums, are readily available.

Finally, be sure to promote your demonstration effectively using a variety of channels, including social media, email, and word of mouth. This can help generate enthusiasm and build momentum for your cause, while also ensuring that your target audience is aware of the demonstration.

Managing crowd dynamics

Protests can be powerful tools for expressing dissent and demanding change, but they can also be dangerous and unpredictable events. Managing crowd dynamics is therefore a crucial aspect of organizing and participating in protests, as it can help ensure the safety of all involved and the effectiveness of the demonstration.

One of the most important factors in managing crowd dynamics is communication. Protest organizers should have clear and effective channels for communicating with participants, including social media, email lists, and group messaging apps. They should also provide information about the protest route, starting location, and any potential hazards or risks. This can help participants feel informed and prepared, and can also help organizers maintain control over the crowd.

Another important aspect of managing crowd dynamics is ensuring that there are enough trained marshals or stewards on hand to help guide the crowd and ensure safety. These marshals should be identifiable by their clothing or armbands, and should be trained in basic crowd management techniques, such as forming human chains to prevent people from entering dangerous areas or helping to manage traffic flow.

It is also important to have a plan for dealing with potential disruptions or conflicts. Protest organizers should have clear protocols in place for handling situations such as counter-protests, violent behavior, or police interference. This may include establishing designated safe spaces for protesters, creating a system for reporting incidents, and having legal resources available to offer support if necessary.

In addition to these measures, it is important for protesters themselves to be aware of their surroundings and the behavior of those around them. Participants should be encouraged to look out for each other and to report any potentially dangerous or disruptive behavior to marshals or organizers. They should also be prepared to adapt to changing circumstances, such as unexpected changes in the protest route or the presence of law enforcement.

Finally, it is important for protest organizers and participants to remember that managing crowd dynamics is an ongoing process that requires ongoing vigilance and attention. While a well-planned and well-executed protest can be a powerful tool for social change, it is important to be prepared for the unexpected and to be ready to adapt to changing circumstances in order to ensure the safety and effectiveness of the demonstration. By working together and staying alert, protesters can help to create a safe and empowering environment for all involved.

Responding to counter-protesters or unexpected events

Protests can be powerful vehicles for social change, but they can also be unpredictable events that can sometimes lead to confrontation or conflict. One of the most common challenges that protesters face is the presence of counter-protesters or unexpected events that can disrupt the demonstration. In such situations, it is important for protest organizers and participants to be prepared to respond in a way that maximizes safety and effectiveness.

One of the key strategies for responding to counter-protesters or unexpected events is to have a clear plan in place. Protest organizers should have a designated point person or team who is responsible for monitoring the situation and responding to any incidents. They should also have clear protocols in place for communicating with participants, marshals, and law enforcement, and should provide regular updates on the situation.

In situations where counter-protesters are present, it is important for protesters to remain calm and avoid engaging in verbal or physical confrontations. Instead, protesters should focus on staying united and maintaining a peaceful presence. Marshals or stewards can help to guide the crowd away from potential conflicts and keep a safe distance between the two groups.

In situations where unexpected events occur, such as the sudden appearance of law enforcement or the discovery of a hazardous object or substance, protest organizers should follow established protocols for responding to such incidents. This may involve designating a safe space for protesters to gather, communicating with participants about the situation, and working with law enforcement or other authorities to ensure the safety of all involved.

It is also important for protest organizers and participants to be aware of their legal rights and responsibilities. They should have a clear understanding of local laws and regulations related to protests, as well as any relevant permits or other documentation required for the demonstration. They should also be prepared to assert their rights in a peaceful and non-violent manner, and to seek legal assistance if necessary.

Finally, it is important for protest organizers and participants to remain flexible and adaptable in the face of unexpected events. While it is important to have a plan in place, it is also important to be prepared to modify that plan as needed in response to changing circumstances. By working together and remaining vigilant, protesters can help to create a safe and effective demonstration that promotes positive social change.

Following Through

Evaluating the success of the protest

Evaluating the success of a protest is an important part of the organizing process, as it can help protesters to understand the impact of their efforts and identify areas for improvement in future demonstrations. However, measuring the success of a protest can be a complex and multifaceted process that requires careful consideration of a variety of factors.

One of the most obvious measures of success for a protest is the size of the turnout. A large number of participants can help to demonstrate the level of support for the cause, and can also help to attract media attention and raise public awareness. However, the size of the crowd alone is not always an accurate indicator of success, as a smaller demonstration can still have a significant impact if it is well-organized and effectively executed.

Another key factor in evaluating the success of a protest is the extent to which it achieved its stated goals. Protest organizers should have clear and measurable objectives for the demonstration, such as advocating for a specific policy change or raising awareness about a particular issue. They should also have a plan for measuring the success of the protest in relation to these goals, such as tracking media coverage or monitoring public opinion.

The effectiveness of the protest message is also an important consideration when evaluating its success. Protesters should strive to communicate a clear and compelling message that resonates with the public and generates support for the cause. This may involve developing a clear and concise message, utilizing social media and other communication channels to amplify the message, and developing creative and attention-grabbing protest tactics.

Finally, the impact of the protest on the broader social and political landscape should also be taken into account when evaluating its success. A successful protest can help to shift public opinion, generate media attention, and even influence policy decisions. It can also help to build momentum for future demonstrations and create a sense of community and solidarity among protesters.

Ultimately, evaluating the success of a protest requires a holistic and nuanced approach that takes into account a wide range of factors. Protest organizers should be thoughtful and intentional in their planning and evaluation efforts, and should strive to learn from each demonstration in order to improve their tactics and strategies in the future. By doing so, they can help to create more effective and impactful protests that promote positive social change.

Maintaining momentum and engagement

Maintaining momentum and engagement is a critical component of successful protests, as sustained public pressure is often necessary to achieve meaningful social change. However, keeping protesters engaged and motivated over the long term can be a challenge, as people's attention spans can be limited and competing demands on their time and resources can arise.

One strategy for maintaining momentum and engagement is to develop a clear and compelling message that resonates with the public and inspires people to take action. This may involve developing a well-crafted narrative that highlights the urgency and importance of the cause, as well as utilizing social media and other communication channels to amplify the message and engage a wider audience.

Another key strategy is to develop a range of tactics and activities that can help to sustain public interest and engagement. This may involve organizing rallies, marches, and other public events, as well as developing creative and attention-grabbing protest tactics that generate media attention and generate interest from the public.

Engaging with local communities and building partnerships with other organizations and groups can also help to maintain momentum and engagement. By building coalitions and working collaboratively with other stakeholders, protesters can help to amplify their message and build broader public support for their cause.

Protest organizers should also be strategic in their use of resources and time, focusing their efforts on high-impact activities that can help to drive meaningful change. This may involve developing clear and achievable goals, and tracking progress toward these goals over time in order to maintain a sense of momentum and progress.

Finally, protesters should be intentional about cultivating a sense of community and belonging among participants. This may involve creating opportunities for people to connect with each other and build relationships, as well as providing support and resources to help participants stay engaged and motivated over the long term.

In conclusion, maintaining momentum and engagement is essential for successful protests, and requires careful planning, strategic thinking, and a commitment to sustained effort over time. By developing a clear and compelling message, utilizing a range of tactics and activities, building partnerships and community, and remaining focused on achievable goals, protesters can help to create sustained public pressure that drives meaningful social change.

Planning next steps and ongoing activism

Planning next steps and ongoing activism is a critical aspect of effective protest movements, as sustained effort is often required to achieve lasting social change. However, developing a clear and actionable plan for ongoing activism can be a challenging task, as it requires careful consideration of a wide range of factors and the development of a long-term strategy for sustained engagement.

One key strategy for planning next steps and ongoing activism is to build on the momentum generated by the initial protest event. This may involve developing a series of follow-up events and activities that help to sustain public interest and engagement, such as rallies, marches, and other public events. It may also involve building partnerships and coalitions with other organizations and groups, and leveraging these partnerships to drive ongoing advocacy and activism efforts.

Another important aspect of planning next steps and ongoing activism is to develop a clear and measurable set of goals and objectives. This may involve identifying specific policy changes or social outcomes that the protest movement aims to achieve, as well as developing clear benchmarks for tracking progress toward these goals over time. By developing clear and achievable goals, protesters can help to maintain a sense of momentum and progress, and keep participants motivated and engaged over the long term.

It is also important to consider the role of education and community-building in ongoing activism efforts. Protest movements can serve as powerful tools for raising public awareness and building community, and ongoing activism efforts should be designed to build on this momentum and promote continued learning and engagement among participants. This may involve developing educational resources and materials, hosting workshops and training sessions, and creating opportunities for participants to connect with each other and build relationships.

Finally, it is essential to remain adaptable and responsive to changing circumstances and new opportunities for advocacy and activism. Effective protest movements must be willing to shift their focus and tactics as needed in response to changing political and social landscapes, and remain committed to sustained effort over the long term.

In conclusion, planning next steps and ongoing activism is a critical aspect of effective protest movements, and requires careful consideration of a wide range of factors and the development of a long-term strategy for sustained engagement. By building on momentum generated by the initial protest event, developing clear goals and objectives, promoting education and community-building, and remaining adaptable and responsive to changing circumstances, protesters can help to create sustained public pressure that drives meaningful social change over time.

Conclusion

Reflections on the importance of protest

Protest is a critical tool for promoting social change and driving progress on a wide range of issues. From civil rights and gender equality to environmental justice and economic opportunity, protest has played a key role in advancing important social and political movements throughout history.

One of the key reasons why protest is so important is that it provides a mechanism for marginalized and disenfranchised communities to have their voices heard and their concerns addressed. Through collective action and public demonstration, protesters can shine a light on important issues and demand accountability from those in power. This can help to build public awareness and support for important causes, and drive meaningful policy changes and social outcomes.

Protest also serves as a powerful form of community-building and empowerment. By coming together in shared cause, protesters can build solidarity and support networks, and create a sense of shared identity and purpose. This can be particularly important for marginalized communities that have historically been excluded from political and social power structures.

Furthermore, protest can serve as a means of holding institutions and individuals accountable for their actions. By shining a light on injustice and demanding accountability, protesters can help to expose wrongdoing and drive meaningful change in a wide range of contexts.

At the same time, protest is not without its challenges and risks. Protests can be emotionally and physically draining, and participants may face harassment, violence, or other forms of intimidation from those who oppose their message. Protesters must also navigate complex legal and regulatory frameworks that can limit their ability to demonstrate and speak out effectively.

Despite these challenges, however, protest remains a vital tool for driving meaningful social change and promoting justice and equity. By working together and remaining committed to sustained effort over the long term, protesters can help to build a more just and equitable world for all.

Appendices:

Glossay

Activism: The act of campaigning or working to bring about social or political change.

Civil disobedience: A non-violent form of protest where individuals refuse to obey certain laws or rules in order to draw attention to an unjust system.

Counter-protest: A protest staged in response to another protest, often with opposing views.

Direct action: A form of protest that involves taking direct and often disruptive action to bring about change.

Free speech: The right to express one's views without censorship, restraint, or fear of retribution.

Nonviolent resistance: A form of protest that is characterized by the use of nonviolent tactics, such as civil disobedience, to effect change.

Organizing: The process of planning and coordinating actions or events in order to bring about social or political change.

Police brutality: The use of excessive force by police officers, including violence, harassment, and intimidation.

Protest: A public expression of dissent or opposition to a particular issue or policy, often involving a public demonstration or march.

Solidarity: Unity or agreement of feeling or action, especially among individuals with a common interest or purpose.

Systemic racism: Racism that is embedded within the social, economic, and political systems of a society, rather than simply being the result of individual biases or prejudices.

Unrest: Social or political disturbance, often characterized by protests, strikes, or other forms of public disruption.

Vigil: A public gathering or demonstration, often held in memory of a person or group that has experienced injustice or tragedy.

Woke: A term used to describe a heightened awareness and understanding of social and political issues, often used to describe individuals or groups that are actively engaged in social justice activism.

Resources for further reading and activism

For those interested in learning more about protests and activism, there are a wealth of resources available to explore. Whether you are new to activism or a seasoned protester, these resources can help to deepen your understanding of the history and theory of protest, as well as provide practical tips and guidance for planning and executing effective demonstrations.

Books are a great place to start when it comes to learning about protest and activism. Some notable titles include "Rules for Radicals" by Saul Alinsky, which provides a framework for organizing and mobilizing grassroots movements; "The Autobiography of Malcolm X," which documents the life and work of one of the most important civil rights leaders of the 20th century; and "This Changes Everything" by Naomi Klein, which explores the relationship between capitalism and the environment and provides a call to action for climate justice activists.

In addition to books, there are a wealth of online resources available to those interested in learning more about protest and activism. Online platforms such as Change.org,

MoveOn.org, and Color of Change provide tools and resources for organizing and mobilizing campaigns, while websites such as Black Lives Matter and the Women's March provide information about ongoing activism efforts and resources for those looking to get involved.

Social media can also be a powerful tool for connecting with other activists and staying up-to-date on the latest protests and demonstrations. Platforms such as Twitter, Instagram, and Facebook can be used to share information, coordinate actions, and amplify the voices of marginalized communities.

Finally, it can be helpful to seek out local resources and organizations that are focused on activism and social justice. Local community centers, advocacy groups, and nonprofits can provide valuable information and resources for those interested in getting involved in local protests and campaigns.

Overall, the key to effective activism and protest is education, organization, and community building. By learning about the history and theory of protest, connecting with other activists and organizations, and taking concrete action to effect change, individuals can make a meaningful impact on the world around them.